SPRING QUARTER ISSUE 6

COVER IMAGE
PASTOR LENARD AND LISA TILLERY

GRAPHIC DESIGNER
LIVING WATER BOOKS

EDITOR
LaDEIDRE MARIS EDITOR IN CHIEF

LIVING WATER MAGAZINE STAFF
TINA TOLBERT
BRIEON GOLDSMITH
ASHA CANNON
BIANCA GRADNEY
TYNESHIA WARREN
JALISHA HILL
CAROLYN OLANIYI
CRYSTALYN MASON

MARKETING
LIVING WATER BOOKS ADVERTISEMENT AND MARKETING
CHARLES MARIS

EMAIL: LIVINGWATERBOOKSGRAPHICSANDDESIGNS@GMAIL.COM

LIVINGWATERBOOKS.ORG

PUBLISHED QUARTERLY BY LIVING WATER BOOKS PUBLISHING INC.

LIVINGWATER
Christian Magazine — John 7:38

Welcome

It is our pleasure to introduce the voice of God, creativity, passion, excitement, and information throughout the pages of this magazine. Many see the bible as one big book filled with inspiring promises. Still, it's many books written by different authors organized to help us understand the nature of God and his people. God is a creative writer who writes his word in the hearts of His people. We are excited to launch a place where God can inspire and draw others to him through your story.

And I, if I am lifted from the earth, will draw all men to Myself. (John 12:32)

"Living Waters Magazine" provides a platform for God's handiwork. It is where writers can express their passions, share their stories from God, and blossom in their anointing as scribes.

Scribes in the earth..... You have been chosen!

> **WE ARE HERE TO ADVANCE THE KINGDOM OF GOD**

THE EMPTY STOCKING

BRENDA

My mother, Brenda Warren, died in 2015. She left her journal to me and her words from God live on to impact others. She is a founding member of Living Water Books still

Move Forward

From The Journals of My Mother
Rest in Love

What happened in the past is not as important as your future. Let go of the hurt and pain of the past. You can give yourself a better future by moving forward. God will be right there with you. Your future has so much in store,

- learn to travel light,
- forgive quickly
- shake off disappointment.

If someone mistreats you, just know that their actions cannot defeat you. Never let life struggles get you down. Life is not over because you lost a loved one. If you replay the negative emotions repeatedly, it will be hard to heal, but you must. You must move forward. Have a strong will, a fighting desire, and a passionate heart to move forward.

- How long will you mourn?
- How long will you weep?

What you think is a stumbling block is actually a stepping stone. Don't live life looking in the rearview mirror. It will never be what it used to be. It will be better. Trust me, I know now. MOVE FORWARD!

CONTENTS

09

23

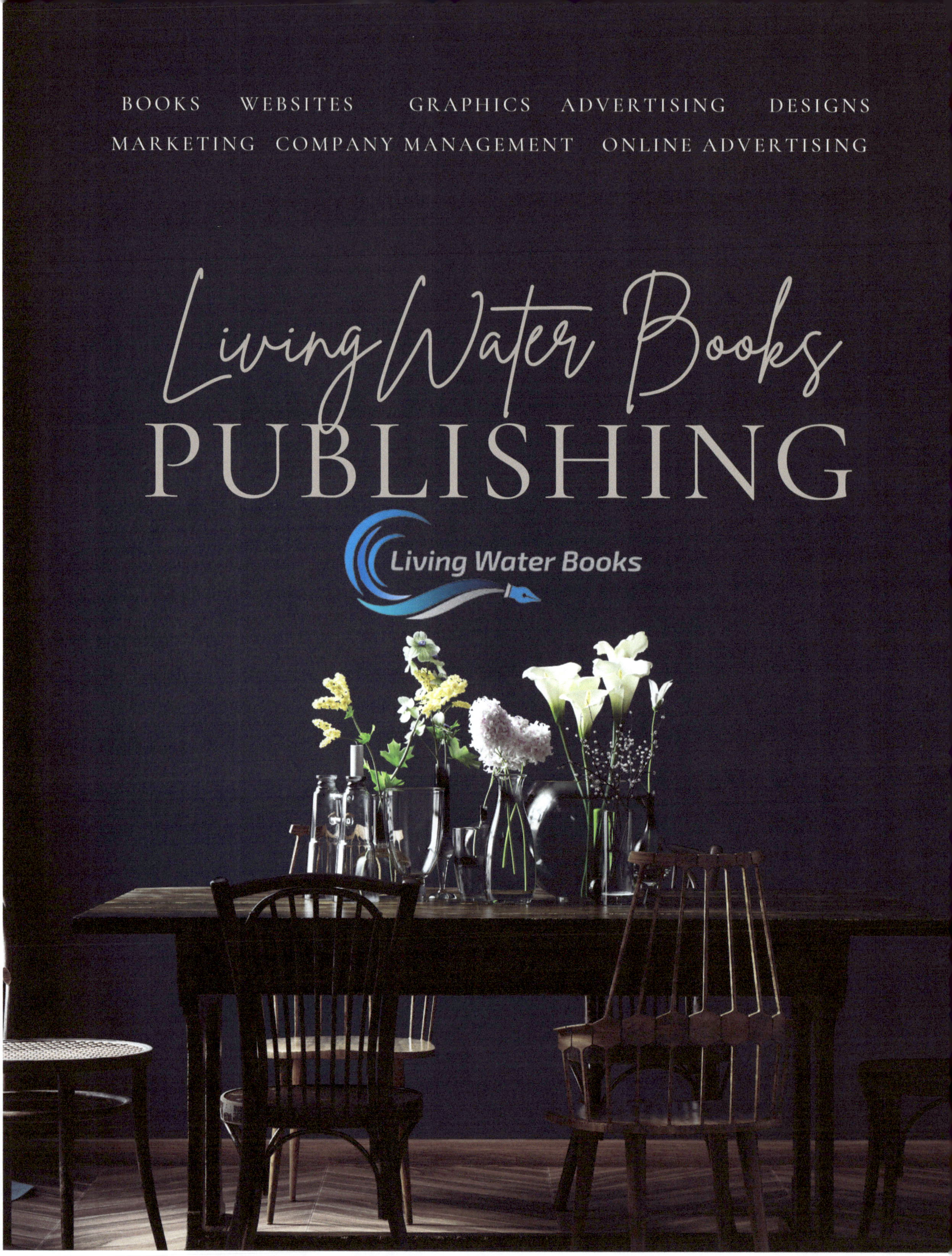
BOOKS WEBSITES GRAPHICS ADVERTISING DESIGNS
MARKETING COMPANY MANAGEMENT ONLINE ADVERTISING
Living Water Books
PUBLISHING
Living Water Books

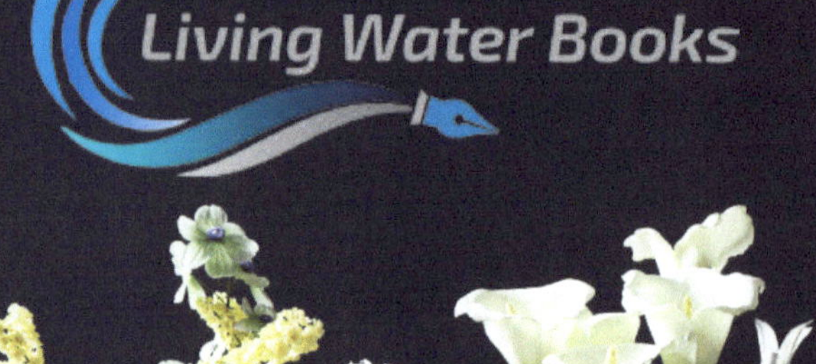

WE PUBLISH

BOOKS

DIGITAL BOOKS

CHILDREN BOOKS

PLANNERS

JOURNALS

NOTEBOOKS

TEXT BOOKS

WE DESIGN

ALBUM COVERS

POSTERS

FLYERS

PLOGOS

SOCIAL MEDIA COVERS

POSTCARDS

PHAMPLETS

WE ADVERTISE

COMPANY ADS

ONLINE ADVERTISEMENT

PRINT ADS

GOOGLE ADS

YOUTUBE ADS

BUILD BRAND

SOCIAL MEDIA PAGES

COMPANY MANAGEMENT

CONTACT US   1-833-777-1180

LIVINGWATERBOOKS.ORG

Global Impact

SCHOOL OF MINISTRY
& ACCREDITED BIBLE COLLEGE

Designed by God to Unveil a Generation of End Time Anointed Men and Women of God

- 2-YEAR ASSOCIATE DEGREE PROGRAM
- 4-YEAR BACHELOR'S DEGREE PROGRAM

- LICENSING AND ORDINATION
- ONLINE DIVINITY PROGRAM
- CHAPLAINCY PROGRAM

FOUNDER APOSTLE BRENDA JEFFERSON

Contact us: https://tinyurl.com/GlobalImpactEnrollment

9900 BROCKINGTON ROAD
SHERWOOD, ARKANSAS 72120
ENROLL TODAY (501)-834-5477

BURN OUT

SELF CARE–DO IT FOR THEM

Are you loving, caring, compassionate, charitable or merciful? Answering yes to any of these adjectives probably places you close to the top of the list when it comes to "occupational burn out.."

COLUMNIST
AUTHOR DR. LOU TURNER

The World Health Organization (WHO) identifies occupational burnout resulting from chronic work-related stress. Symptoms include: "exhaustion, feelings of energy depletion, increased mental distance from one's job, or feelings of negativism related to one's job." (wikipedia.org) Dr. Herbert Freudenberger's book, "Burn out: the high cost of high achievement;"

Your self-care will look different from others!

You could be heading for burn out if any of the above applies to you.

Dr. Freudenberger defined burn out as a state of mental and physical exhaustion caused by one's professional life. He is the originator of the term burn out. As the kind, caring compassionate person you probably have many referrals. Of course your reputation for going the extra mile to help others gets word of mouth publicity. You become the go-to person for needs in your area of expertise and perhaps other areas. The proverbial "straw that broke the angels back" actually refers to an accumulation of unresolved stress and the end result.

Are you among the following?

- 1. Are you working more now and enjoying it less? (On job, at the marriage, in friendshi8p or love)?

- 2. Do you find it more difficult to confide in others?

- 3. Must you force yourself to do routine things?

- 4. Are you listless, bored, or constantly seeking excitement?

- 5. Would you rather be somewhere else?(doing something else with someone else).

- 6. Have you lost the joy of sex?

- 7. Do you drink more than you used to? (Even if it's only one)

- 8. Do you need a tranquilizer to face the day? A sleeping pill to get through the night?

- 9. Are you resigned about your future?

- 10. Is your need for a particular clutch increasing? (smoking eating, nail-biting, pot)

We might say it another way, "it got on my last nerve." Either way there is a reference to a breaking point with an explanation, "I just couldn't take anymore". You need a management strategy to avoid occupational burnout. Consider, as a foundation, the establishment of boundaries. Simply put, boundaries represent limitations. Ask yourself, what limitations have I placed on access to my time, talents, and help? Do you make it easy for others to invade your scheduled or unscheduled 'personal recharging' time? Have you clarified your meaning of "this is an emergency"?

As a young mother of three facing burn out that affected my relationship with my children Holy Spirit gave me specific instructions. At the time I did not see the big picture. I was to have at least one place in our home designated as my recharging station. When in that place I was not to be disturbed. I took no phone calls, I answered no questions and I did not emerge except for emergencies. The strategy applied to family and friends. What an awesome self-care strategy for me. My job was wife and mother.

Your self-care plan may look very different. Each strategy should take into consideration the occupation. Can you put your mobile phone on 'do not disturb' for one hour? As Believers, Saints of God, offspring of the Living God, and citizens of the kingdom of God, we have the Spirit of God living inside. That Spirit produces fruit that is not for us. It is for others, the body of Christ, and others we encounter. That fruit is identified in Galatians 5:22-23 as Love, joy, peace, long-suffering, gentleness, goodness, faith, meekness, and temperance.

If we have reached a place psychologically where we are unable to control our anger, now the spiritual fruit has to work extremely hard to press through to be a blessing to others. How could any of the following affect your ability to be a blessing: depression, frequent illness, temper outbursts? These are just a few symptoms that can be categorized as psychological, physical, and behavioral.

KNOW WHEN
YOUR BOUNDARY
HAS BEEN VIOLATED

The Bible gives us an account of Moses being counseled by his father-in-law to let qualified people help him. A principle here is, care for others and be cared for by others. Listen to Jesus. He knew when unplanned virtue had left His body.

In Luke 8:46, "And Jesus said Somebody touched me: for I perceive that virtue is gone out of me." The indication here is when His boundary had been violated, Jesus was aware. Because He knows everything, consider that He used this as a teaching moment. We can only speculate that He took the necessary steps for recharging.

The principle to be realized is to know when our boundary has been violated and address it with love. As vessels of the Holy Spirit, we are valuable to the body of Christ and the world. Engage in wholistic self-care. Do it for them.

Dr. Lou Turner

LETTER TO GOD

AUTHOR TINA TOLBERT
A DAY ALONE WITH GOD

I'm at the lake again holding my signature pen while writing my thoughts to you again and allowing them to ascend.

I'm here to let you know I need your Holy Spirit to guide me again as your dear friend.

I look in awe at the Wonders you made the scenery at the lake is so serene.
Oh!! how I just love to hear the birds sing melodies of praises to you.

THE CREATOR, THE ONE THATS TRUE.

I love to feel the fresh wind blow kisses on my face as I remember how much I desire your love and grace.

I smile because of the peace I feel as I look at the ripples of water dancing with the rays of the sun.

The lake is my secret place where I come to talk with you. I can tell you everything and I know you hear my cry.

I'm able to stand on the earth with my barefoot and feel your energy flow through me. I become centered, focused and grounded at the lake with you.

Dear God, I just love you.

WWW.ASHLETICSFITNESSWEAR.COM
SHARRIKA
ASHLEY JOHNSON
OWNER
JOIN US NOW
BUILD YOUR BODY
ASHLETICS
FITNESS
WEAR

WHAT INFLUENCES YOUR LIFE, GIVES YOU MOTIVATION TO CONTINUE?

The impact I have on others, my journey it took to get there, the health issues that runs in my family, determination, commitment and choosing me is the most positive thing that influences my life.

HOW DOES FITNESS POSITIVELY INFLUENCE YOUR LIFE?

I was always told that if you take care of your body, it will take care of you. I use to see myself everyday fit and healthy and that along kept me grounded and motivated to continue my health journey.

WHAT WOULD YOU RECOMMEND TO OTHERS WHO WANT TO BE FIT AND HEALTHY?

I would say,
- Clear your mind
- Get motivated
- Be determined
- Stay dedicated
- Always find time for you, which is the gym.
- Don't go to the gym with anyone. Why?

You will find yourself quitting on their schedule.

Facebook Ashletics Fitness Wear

Instagram Ashletics Fitness Wear

TikTok Ashletics Fitness Wear

> Les Brown states: "You have to make a commitment and stick with your commitment. If it's hard then do it hard but always keep your commitment to your commitment."

Oily Prayers

Journalist Crystalyn Mason

Oily prayers are prayers that are anointed
and brings forth Heaven on Earth.!

1 Thessalonians states Rejoice always, pray without ceasing, in everything give thanks; for this is the will of God in Christ Jesus for you. How is all of this the will of God for you through Christ Jesus?

Let's consider the first one listed, which is to rejoice always. Looking at the word, we see the root word being Joy! This Joy is from the Holy Spirit, which is a fruit that grows on the vine according to Galatians 5:22. The second is to pray without ceasing, meaning pray without stopping; It's continual, just as oil; according to 2Kings4, the widow has a continuous flow of oil. Oily prayers aren't nonchalant or mundane; they are bold and purposeful. The Bible says, 'Let us, therefore, come boldly to the throne of grace, that we may obtain mercy and find grace to help in time of need.' Hebrews 4:16

> *"Prayers must be bold because*
> *God responds to his word."*

Oily prayers are anointed words from God that grab the attention of God. "Jesus" is a powerful prayer that carries weight no matter what you're facing. Jesus was found seeking God and thus carried oily prayers to the secret place on the Mount of Olives. This place is so significant because of the weight of Jesus' prayers in the garden! Jesus prayed, saying, "Father, if it is your will, take this cup away from me; nevertheless, not my will, but yours, be done." Luke 22:42. How often do we go into the throne room of grace praying for our will instead of praying for God's will to be done in us?

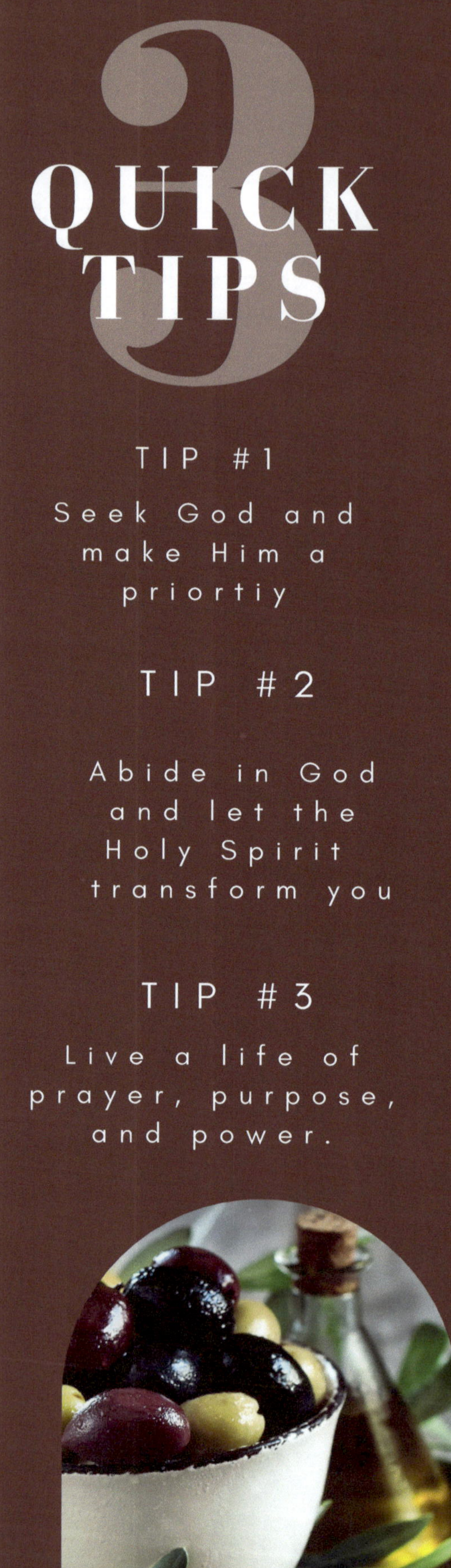

Jesus' prayers were oily because they always brought about miraculous results! Oily prayers are those where we are intentional about praying, spending time with God, and getting to know His heart!

When we pray the will of God, the anointing of God falls fresh upon us and penetrates the atmosphere. These prayers open the doorway to the Father's heart and bring forth change. The scriptures say, 'But you, when you pray, go into your room, and when you have shut your door, pray to your Father who is in the secret place; and your Father who sees in secret will reward you openly.' Matthew 6:6.

This is what Jesus did; he drew into the secret chambers and prayed, coupled with fasting. God wants us to have our own Mount Of Olives experience. This place, the Mount of Olives, was where Jesus was called to be alone, have quiet time, sit, reflect, and hear the voice of God. When He heard the voice of God, He heard the heart of the Father, and this is what it means to know God's will. We often wonder, "What's God's will for my life?" The other standing question is, how many times have we gone into our own Mount of Olives to "press in" and hear God? The Mount of Olives was also known as the Garden of Gethsemane, which also means "oil press." Jesus went in, and the burden of the cross pressed Him in a spiritual sense that He had to go to the Father for help. Jesus knew where His help came from. He sweats drops of blood because the burden was so great within Him. Now let's go to the vine; how does the vine have anything to do with oily prayers? Olives grow on the vine just as a fruit, now look at this spiritually because the olive being Jesus Himself and the sweat drops of blood would be symbolic to the juice that comes from an olive when it is crushed! This is an intentional posture.

"My food is to do the will of the Father. The oil flows in that place."

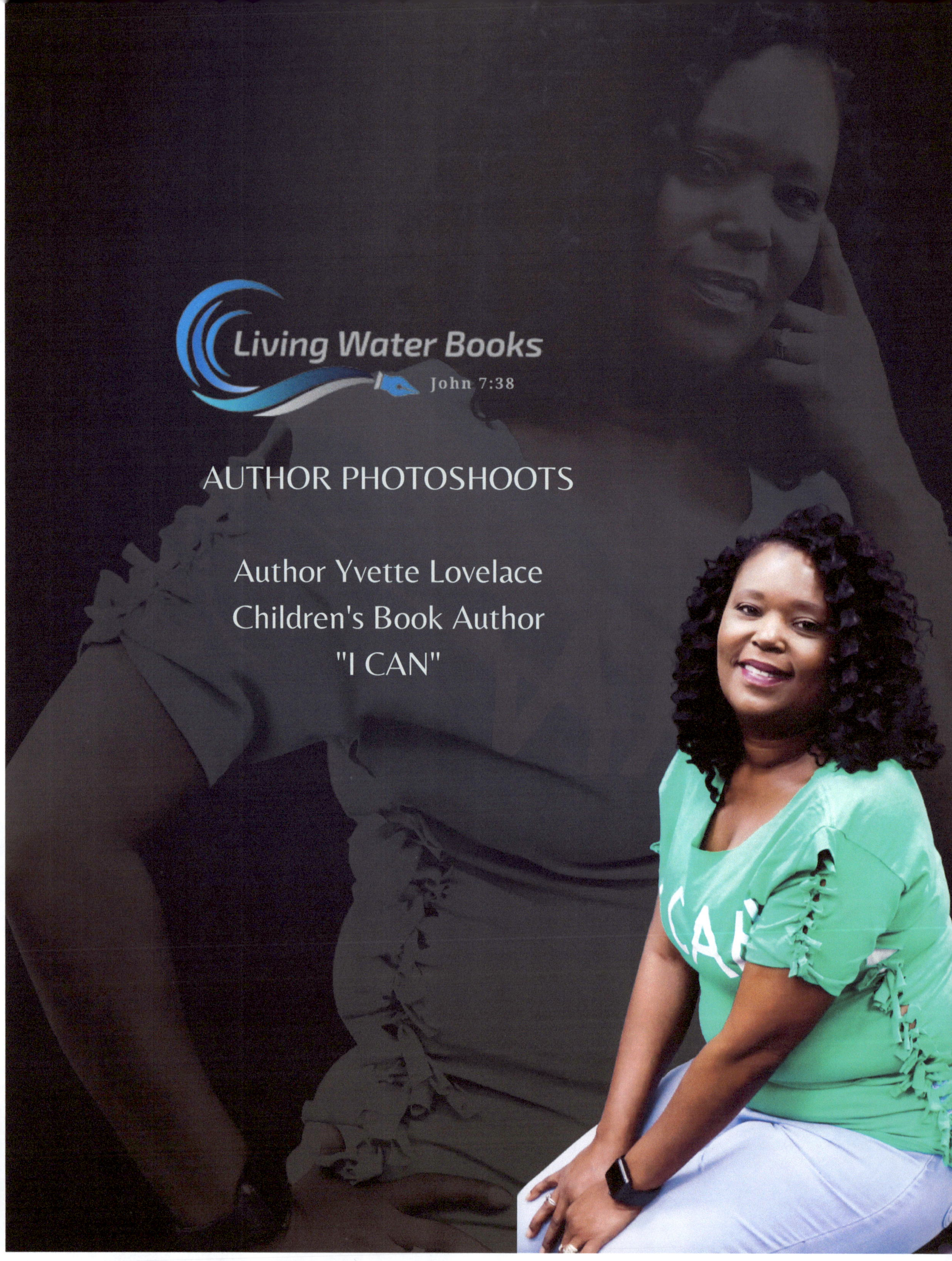

Living Water Books
John 7:38

AUTHOR PHOTOSHOOTS

Author Yvette Lovelace
Children's Book Author
"I CAN"

I CAN
COMING
SOON
By: Author Yvette Lovelace
I CAN

SURELY GOD WILL SUSTAIN ME

PSALM 54:4
Journalist Bianca Gradney

Surely God is my help; the Lord is the one who sustains me.

As a seventh grader in middle school, I found solace in writing. I wanted to be heard and seen as a child, but due to many reasons, I wasn't. I would do many things to get what I desired from my parents, some good and bad. I remember one particular day; I wrote a poem about a suicide attempt that was so vivid in my mind as if I saw it in a movie. I wrote it as if I was speaking in the third person. After finishing up the final touches, I enthusiastically ran to show my mom and sister with great hopes that this would open the dialogue so that they would join in and discuss the thoughts I was having. In disappointment, I received compliments for how great my poem was, but to my surprise, it wasn't alarming to them that I would even construct a poem about a severe topic at my age. I was devastated that I still had not found the solution to what seemed like a never-ending cycle that could one day mean the end of my life. Many years went by, and my thoughts began to turn into attempts. I started noticing a pattern. Still, I struggled to identify the core reason and how to make it disappear. There were times I attempted to take my life, and I could recall blacking out. As I was brought into the hospital on a stretcher, I cried to God to give me another chance and prevent me from going to Hell. I was raised in a church where I was spiritually abused. The abuse came from one of the leaders of the church. I thought she could be trusted since the pastor appointed her.

He said Because you are chosen !! I cried, and I cried as His words touched my heart.

I attempted to take my life, but God kept intervening

My lack of knowledge left me questioning God and my identity. I was once again faced with abuse by someone I trusted. It was pretty devastating and traumatic. The memories of the traumatic experience plagued my mind... The bad experience began to take a toll on my mind. The rejection and being under-loved was so overwhelming that it led me back to suicidal thoughts. I remember walking the streets outside as I sat at the bus stop around 3 am. I contemplated suicide right outside, and a homeless stranger talked me out of it. I couldn't help but question God, wondering why He let it happen to me. He spoke to me with a small voice and said, "Because you are chosen." I cried, and I cried as His words touched my heart, but I didn't fully understand the magnitude of His words, and neither did I take the time to explore deeper into what it meant. Afterward, I made many sinful decisions in my search to fill the void I had within due to my lack of feeling loved.

GOD, WHY ARE YOU STOPPING ME?

I searched for love in the wrong places and lost a piece of myself with every decision. Many years later, after getting counseling for the physical abuse. I woke up with anger. Each day I would resent God for what some would see as the gift of life; I saw it as another day to suffer in misery. One morning I woke up with an overwhelming dissatisfaction with my life, so much so that I decided this would be the end.

The plan to take my life became clear as I stared out the window. I rushed downstairs, searching my drawers for my biggest knife. I found it, turned around, and aggressively forced the knife toward my neck, but to my surprise, there was a force more potent than I pushing between my hand holding the knife and my neck. As I continued to push and press, I realized this was God's mighty hand. In frustration, I threw the knife to the floor, looked up at my kitchen ceiling, and screamed, "WHY ARE YOU STOPPING ME!" I heard the Lord say, "Because you still have purpose."

I began to weep because I just couldn't believe God wanted me to live another day with all the pain I felt within. As a backslider returning to God, I knew for sure I had blown it. I knew my life was ruined due to all the wrong choices I made. I wish I could tell you that I never had a suicidal thought after that, but I did. Honestly, the thoughts would come like a monthly cycle. Every time a thought emerged, I found myself running back to God for safety. God began showing me a pattern. Suicidal thoughts would come every time I felt rejected. One day, after experiencing significant pain and rejection, I was driving to a nearby party supply store for my daughter's birthday. As I began to journey toward the store, I couldn't help but worry that the suicidal thoughts were on the way, and just as I had expected, they arrived, but this time so did God in a powerful way.

God said, "You've been dealing with suicidal thoughts since childhood because of your longing to be loved. When others fail to love you, you feel there is no reason to live. I want you to know that the perfect love you seek can only be found in me. I will forever love you, and it is I who sustains you, not people." God's presence and assurance rested on me. I wept right there in the parking lot of Hobby Lobby.

This truth delivered me from believing that I had to rely on others to make it. I no longer had to be codependent. I understood then that because God loves me, I could face whatever comes my way in victory because Christ would strengthen me. I kept the promises of the Lord close as he whispered, "I can do all things through Christ which strengthens me. I shall live and declare the works of the Lord." Today I confidently embrace that God loves me. It has been changing my perspective on many things. I know that it doesn't matter who rejects me because Jesus loves me and accepts me. With God and His Holy Spirit living within me, I know I can make it through anything. Giving up is not an option anymore, for God truly sustains.

GET IT NOW!
WWW.HEISJIREH.COM
I AM
EXCLUSIVE
HEAVENLY COLLECTION
The I AM Who I AM Says I AM Copper Vacuum Insulated Bottle
Founder Avis Wilson
Be lavished in the Love of God
HEISJIREH
I AM
HEAVENLY COLLECTION
Be lavished in the Love of God
WWW.HEISJIREH.COM

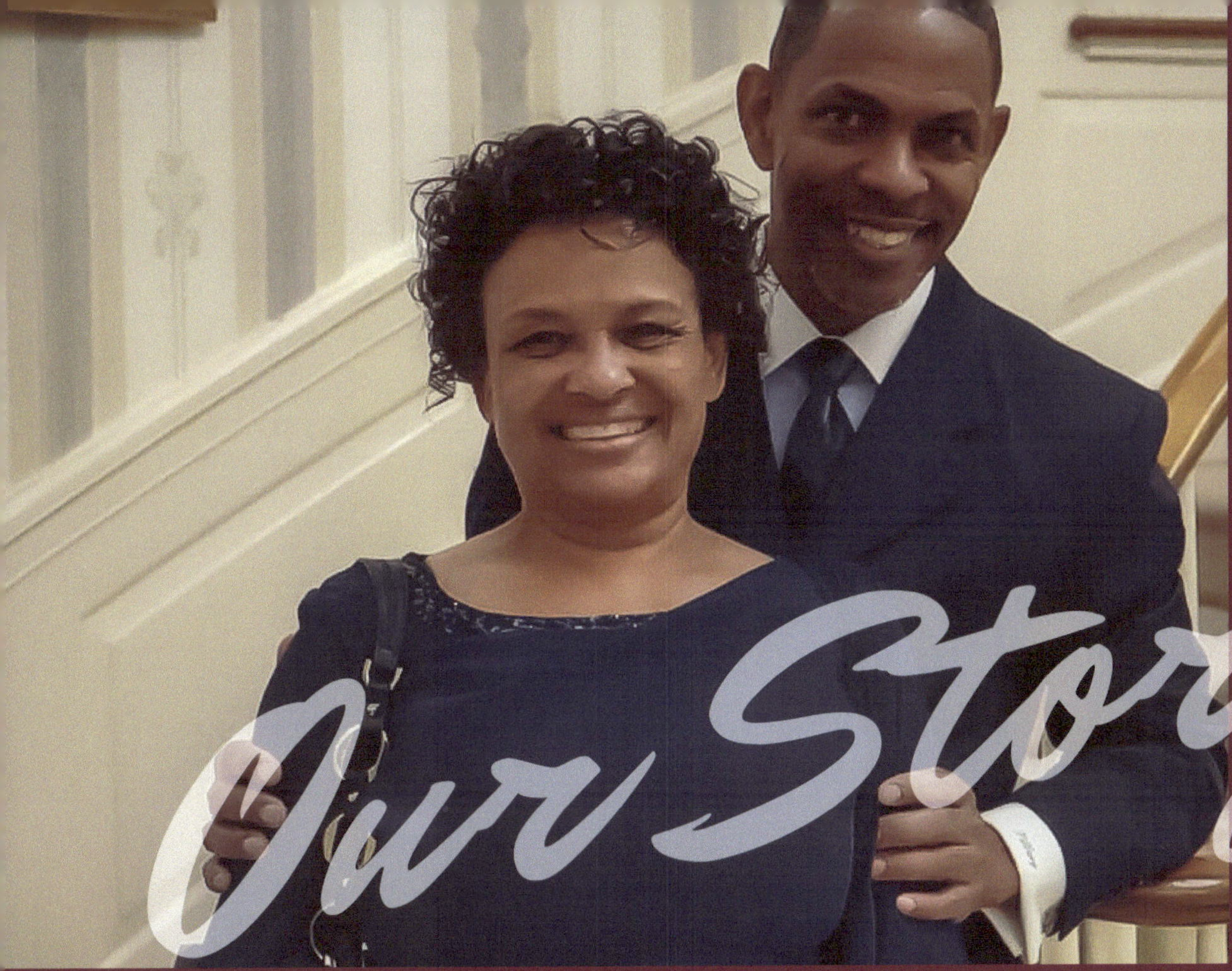

Our Story

PASTOR LENARD AND FIRST LADY LISA TILLERY

THE BEGINNING

In the early days of our marriage, we were so happy to be with each other that we didn't notice the changes and adjustments we were making to make the marriage work. We were in love with each other, in love with the idea of being in love, and, most importantly, in love with God.

The "in love" with God was the common denominator in our love equation that helped us remain grounded through the good and bad events, situations, and circumstances that life sometimes throws our way. We attributed our success in overcoming obstacles and challenges we faced daily by staying positive and seeking to please God.

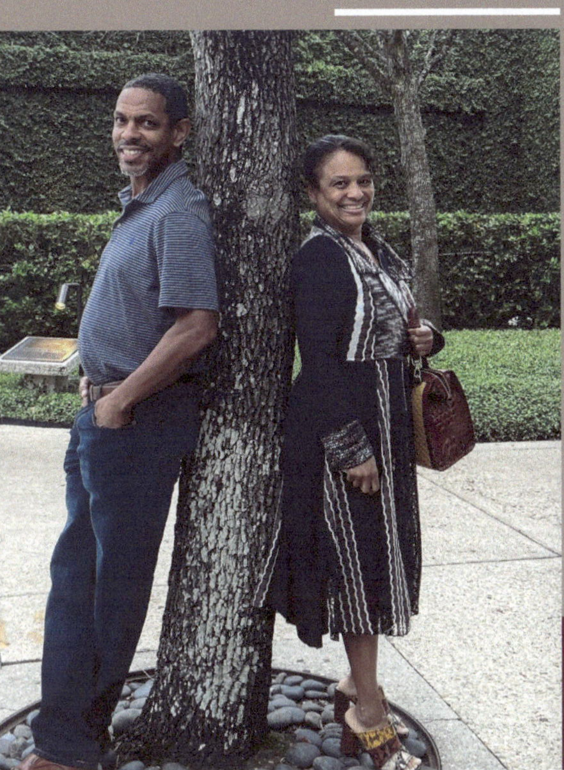

WE REFUSED TO GIVE UP IN THE FACE OF ADVERSITY.

Eventually, the honeymoon stage had several things interjected into it, such as the reality of life, our environment, and each other's differences were revealed. We learned how to communicate better in all areas of our marriage and not to be afraid to say I'm sorry. We maintained our commitment and dedication to each other, and as the years passed, our trust and loyalty to each other grew. We were intentional in our efforts to manage conflict and preserve our "TEAM" mindset despite the daily internal and external pressures surrounding our marriage. We refused to give up in the face of adversity. Our motto that we live by is With God, all things are possible. If we seek his kingdom, everything we need will be added unto us. We embraced the concept of completing each other. We were aware that God created Marriage for Man and Woman to complete each other and not compete with each other.

The more we strived to improve ourselves and grow in our relationship with God, empathy and passion helped us see beyond each other's faults and fulfill each other's needs. The strength of our marriage stemmed from a friendship that developed into a relationship which eventually led to our covenant partnership.

It was at this point we realized the importance and necessity of relationship education and the value the teacher/mentor/counselor role plays in providing not only married couples, but soon-to-be married couples guidance in learning about each other's strengths, weaknesses, values, preferences and personality types. The marriage ministry was forged out of the desire, the burden and the call to share, educate, and equip couples with the knowledge necessary to improve their marriage.

Testimonials

We have endeavored to become visible role models in a generation that doesn't believe in the sanctity of marriage. With the help of God, our marriage will become visible by being an example. Our book, "Marriage Plans for Two" is the next step this generation needs to propel them into a successful, sustainable and happy marriage.

The presentation on communication between couples was a real eye opener.

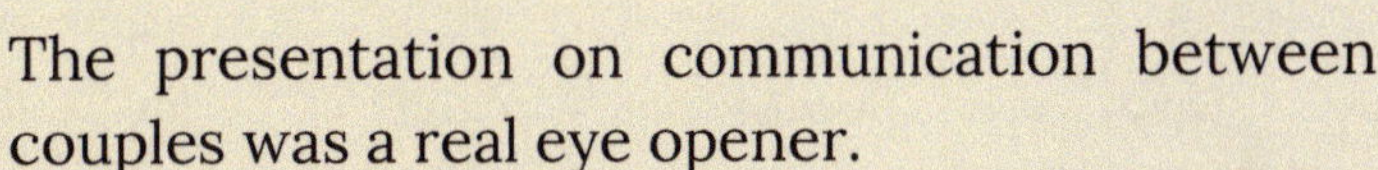

The authenticity of the presenter and the down to earth way the information was presented captured my attention.

I never thought that improving myself could eventually improve my marriage. I never realized that intentionally studying my spouse was so important. And then taking that knowledge and using it in the marriage.

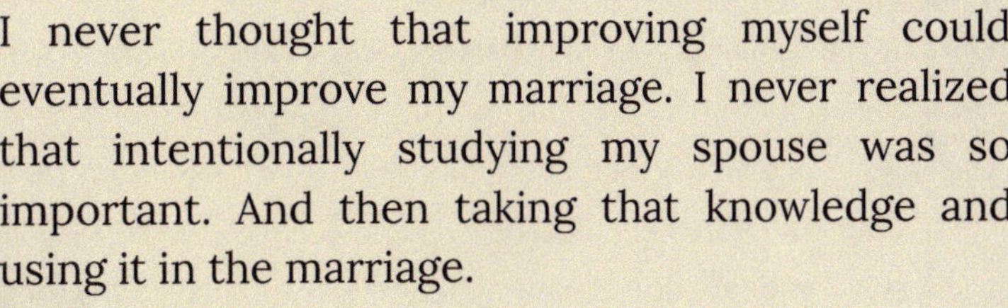

YOU DESERVE EVERYTHING GOD HAS FOR YOU

BUT WILL YOU ACCEPT IT

L can take my rightful place in the Kingdom and the things of God.

I love to serve, and one of my dominant gifts is "Ministry of Helps" (Administration, Hospitality, etc) One day God flipped the script on me. Instead of serving, I was being served!

Talk about uncomfortable... instead of me carrying someone's Bible, I was asked, can I carry your Bible? Can I get you a bottle of water? My husband and I attended a conference in January. The first night we attended, we were met at the door and immediately whisked away into a waiting room with some well-known ministry leaders. Even though I was excited to be among several generals of the faith, I felt out of place, as if I didn't belong. I thank God for the Holy Spirit, who immediately reminded me of the prodigal son. Yes, the prodigal son. We all know the story of how the younger brother left home and lived a reckless life.

Luke 15:21-24 When the son came to "himself," The son said unto him, Father, I have sinned against heaven, and in thy sight, and am no more worthy to be called thy son. But the father said to his servants, "Bring forth the best robe, and put it on him; and put a ring on his hand, and shoes on his feet: bring hither the fatted calf, and kill it, and let us eat, and be merry: For this, my son was dead, and is alive again; he was lost and is found. And they began to be merry.

But, you say, what does this have to do with what happened at the conference? As my Nigerian husband would say, "Wait" I'm coming. I felt unworthy, not because I had sinned, but I felt like these ministers were more "spiritual" than me. God was giving me a "glimpse" of my future, and I didn't feel worthy. See, at that moment, I wasn't thinking of the scripture in Proverbs 18:16, A man's gift makes room for him and brings him before great men. I felt like the prodigal son.

I was thinking servant instead of a son. While there is nothing wrong with serving, that was not what God was doing that night. He was trying to show me my position in the kingdom of God. I love the book of Ephesians; it shows us whom we belong to and what we are. I want to point out Ephesians 2:6, which says, and hath raised us together and made us sit together in heavenly places in Christ Jesus. Wow, did you know you are seated with Christ? Now, that's the position. When we truly know who we are in Christ, we will have the boldness and confidence in him (not in ourselves) to say he is in me, and I am in him. I can take my rightful place in the kingdom and the things of God.

MENTAL HEALTH CHRISTIANITY

Have you ever gone to church Sunday after Sunday, speak the Word over your life regarding healing, and still struggled with mental illness? Have you ever felt like you must have done something wrong? Why were you burdened with depression, anxiety, mood disorders, and eating disorders, or have you ever been diagnosed with schizophrenia or bipolar? They put their hands on you, deliver you and cast demons out… you cry, yell, and everything else, and still…Even in our best efforts to encourage someone struggling, we make them feel worse when we say things like, "God won't put more on you than you can handle!" or "Maybe you haven't fully surrendered your anxiety to God."

Because of various societal factors, there has indeed been an increase in the awareness of mental health because of what we have encountered these past years. Events have heightened the fact that we need to take more care of our mental state. Triggers happen sooner than we expect, and fear and impulsiveness are being pushed at every turn! But as for the Christian – being told to pray about it isn't working. And when you have a Pastor, maybe even church members, or even your own family who won't recognize your illness, can you imagine the hopelessness?

IF GOD SAYS I'M HEALED WHY DO I SUFFER FROM MENTAL ILLNESS

Columnist Asha Cannon

Accepting the facts of mental illness does not mean that we do nothing – or we are just impassive about it. We do what we can to avail ourselves of help and help those struggling. But being a Christian puts us at an advantage more than you know! If you are struggling with mental health concerns, trust me when I say you are not alone, many aren't willing to admit it! Know that God has not cast you down. Many mental illness factors come from situational experiences such as anxiety from an accident or a horrible situation.

It is natural for you to have trauma, and each person is different, so the time it may take you to heal from certain things may differ from others. This is where God's grace comes in like a rushing flood! And as Christians, we should remember to offer the same grace to those as God provides to us. Although we may not be experiencing the same thing, when you are a Christian, the actual evidence is how we show patience, grace, and overwhelming love and support to those. These are the characteristics that also help to heal! When people experience the love of God through their sisters and brothers in Christ, there is hope!

Jeremiah 29:11 says, "For I know the plans I have for you, declares the Lord, plans for welfare and not for evil, to give you a future and a hope." This verse comforts us to know that God is for us, not against us. He has a plan to give me hope and a future, no matter how bad the anxiety may feel like it's trying to take over! This particular verse helps settle anxiousness because even though there may be a very present fear for someone, when you begin to trust and believe this scripture, you know God is with you and already has your life planned.

What better evidence than a host of believers around you rooting for you to be the victor in Christ that you already are? See how I worded that! I spoke life right there into someone. If you are reading this and struggling…know that you are already an overcomer! I know someone may be saying, "Well, I was diagnosed at a young age with schizophrenia." Why would God allow this to be the case? I tell you that God does not make mistakes! You were created with love in His eyes. All who come into this world He knows them before they are even planted in their mother's wombs (Jeremiah 1:5)! The Bible teaches us that in 2 Corinthians 10:5 that we can Cast down imaginations, and every high thing that tries to exalt itself against the knowledge of God, and bringing into captivity every thought to the obedience of Christ.

Your faith can help you transform your thoughts and command them to obey the truth of what you believe! As a Christian, holding on to the belief that no matter what you see, hear, or think, based on God's love and that He designed you for a meaningful purpose means everything will ultimately result in a desirable end! That this to the illness, the anxiety, the diagnosis will pass. Let this notion dominate every thought process and intercept every faulty signal in the brain with this burning faith, and the result WILL BE healed!

If you are reading this and it hit home, know that we are praying for you! Whether it's baby steps, leaps, setbacks, or one day at a time, you have the victory! We love who you are… and so does God!

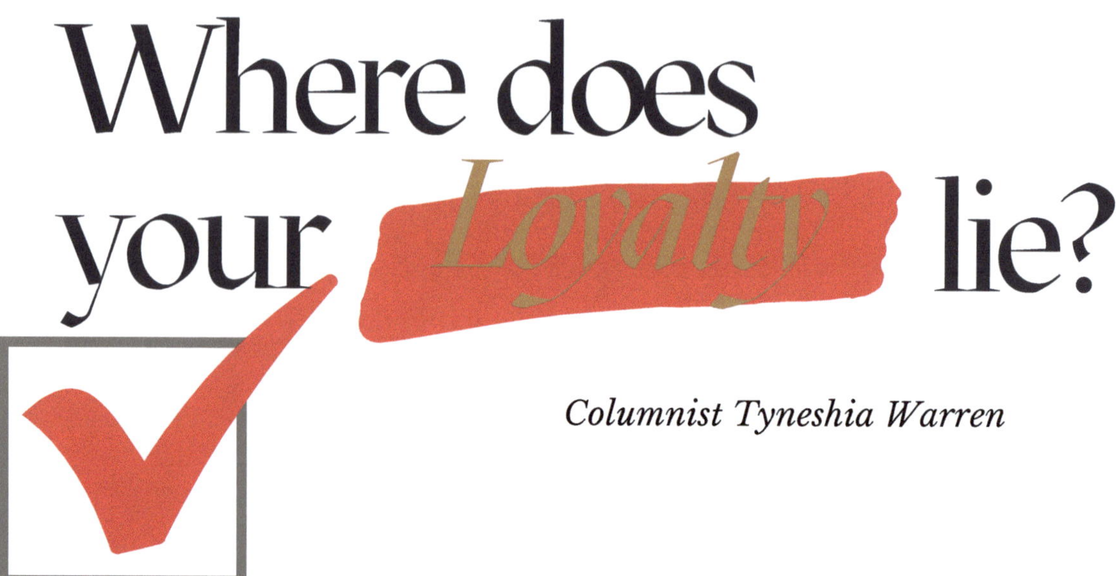

Columnist Tyneshia Warren

**There's nothing wrong
with loyalty except......**

*When you're there for everyone else
yet leave yourself out of the equation*

• • •

In this season of my life, I am constantly asked by the Lord, "Where does your loyalty reside?" My answer has been, "With you, Lord." I had no idea that I had been lying to myself and others around me the whole time.

This year I will be 41. I was so excited about this new chapter that I was embarking upon it until I realized I'd been loyal to everyone else except myself. The Lord gave me an overview of my life and how I have lived over these years.

Anyone who knows me knows that I love my family so much, and I have been loyal to them all my life. Because of my love for them, I have put myself to the side and the dreams the Lord has spoken to me so that I may be there for them. I love extremely hard and unconditionally.

There is nothing wrong with those things except that I leave myself out of the equation. This has been happening for a while. Now I am placed in a position to be loyal to Christ, who dwells in me and to myself, and this has been by far the most challenging task I have ever done, at least it is in my mind.

I recently decided to be loyal to myself and what the Lord calls me to do. You read it right; I had to decide even though the feeling was not present. I am learning to move without emotion and operate in obedience trusting that the feeling will catch up. I also noticed an emptiness inside before the decision, but I assumed it was because my mom and grandmother were no longer present in the flesh. I was wrong; the Lord revealed that the emptiness is from my disobedience. He said I should not build other people's homes and not build my own when the storm comes. Where will you and your children reside if you continue building for others?

I believed that serving others is how my house will be built until the Lord took me to Matthew 25, which speaks about the five wise brides and the five foolish brides. The five wise brides were prepared for the bridegroom, and the five foolish were not prepared. As much as I have been walking with the Lord, I believed I was one of the wise brides until I received this revelation. You can serve all you want, and there is nothing wrong with serving; however, the problem comes when you are serving so much that you are not using your talents the way the Lord asks you to. I assumed that if I focused on myself, I would be considered selfish. This bothered me because I do love giving.

> ## DO SOMETHING TODAY THAT YOUR FUTURE SELF WILL THANK YOU FOR.

Our actions and decisions today will shape the way we will be living in the future.

That was a lie from the enemy I had to come to terms with. I am too much of a giver to be considered selfish. I often gave out of self, intending to be selfless. I quickly realized I needed balance, and I am now receiving that from the Lord every day, all day. There is not a moment that I am not pulling on the Lord for His help regarding this new area, I am in the critical care unit, but I am getting stronger every day. If you are dealing with these things, you should apologize to the Lord for not taking that leap with Him (repentance), forgive yourself, pray for strength, and then decide to be obedient.

Move in complete obedience, and don't sit around having faith with no works. Some steps of obedience may not make sense to you or others but walk in obedience anyways. Trust that it will all come together for those who trust and love the Lord will reap. Be that person trusting and loving the Lord with all your heart, soul, and mind. Don't waiver, be steadfast and immovable. Be in love with your Lord and Savior; he will not disappoint you, but on the other hand, don't get mad at yourself if you have disappointed yourself. It's all about a healthy balance, and I believe that you shall find your balance through obedience to the Lord. I pray that revelation blesses someone the way the Lord blessed and still blesses me with it.

ORDER YOUR COPY
MANEUVERING THROUGH THE OBSTACLE COURSE CALLED LIFE
WALK A MILE in My STILETTOS
CHRISTINA J. BOYKINS

Living Water Books
John 7:38

CONTACT US TODAY

THE CHRISTIAN
PUBLISHING COMPANY

WEBSITE: LIVINGWATERBOOKS.ORG

THE IMPACT A MAN HAS ON A WOMAN

Pastor Charles Maris

"He can love her so deeply healing wounds he didn't cause."

Jesus said, "Greater love has no one than this than to lay down one's life for his friends" (John 15:13 NKJV).

So to imitate Christ on earth, he decides to lay down his life for this special woman. The same gift given to him, he now wants to share with her and no one else. He doesn't want her to compete anymore with another woman or anything else in this world.

I know the impact a man can have on a woman's life whom he plans to marry or is married to when he partners with The Holy Spirit to love her. He can love her so deeply that he can heal wounds he didn't cause as well as those he has caused. He can heal wounds by deciding to make a serious decision to let Christ live through him (Galatians 2:20). Here's the one ingredient needed for this recipe...This man can only do this when he knows God has loved him through the most rebellious years of his life.

When a man thinks about what he himself has needed and what he has done in the sight of God; For God to watch his rebellion and still reach down and get his attention to change his ways, this man will desire to give that same love to the woman he shares his life with and the children God blesses them with. At this point, he realizes God has a great amount of love, mercy, grace, and patience for him.

He now makes a decision to share this love with her, because God's Love is contagious. This world fights so hard for a man's attention, to pull him away from his this special woman, he wants to be in alignment with the Word of God in this one woman's life.

So he lays down his life for hers knowing that when he does this, he can give his cares to God. God will take care of him because his life is now hidden in Christ. Jesus said, "Greater love has no one than this than to lay down one's life for his friends."(John 15:13 NKJV)

So to imitate Christ on earth, he decides to lay down his life for this remarkable woman. The same gift given to him, he now wants to share with her and no one else. He doesn't want her to compete anymore with another woman or anything else in this world.

Emotionally, a woman's emotions can be all over the place, and a husband knows this because he understands the stirring of his own emotions. He partners with Holy Spirit to prevent getting so wrapped up in his own emotions and neglects hers over his own. There is only one person who knows where she is emotionally, spiritually & mentally. He always wants to know where she is so he can provide for whatever needs she may have; this includes but is not limited to

- listening to her cares & concerns,
- being a friend,
- be a lover, or
- just simply being whatever she needs at the moment

Listen, when you can meet a person's needs, you can touch that person's soul. He loves her soul more than her physical body. He loves her soul more than the finances she brings in. He loves her soul more than she could give him. He loves the condition of her soul and spirit because that contributes to her overall well-being. When a woman is healthy emotionally, mentally, & spiritually, she becomes a true biblical helpmeet. She glorifies Christ with how she loves, speaks, and lives out her life. These are just some of the reasons why I wrote The Intune Husband!

Monique Washington is a dedicated author and public speaker who has published over fourteen books and counting which can be found at Barnes & Noble and Amazon. She is a native of Savannah, GA a minister, entrepreneur, speaker, veteran and mentor. Her knack for providing inspiration and encouragement has touched the lives of viewers and listeners all over the US. Monique has been featured in numerous publications and broadcasts to include Voyage ATL Magazine, Younique Magazine, and K Sound Magazine. She has also founded her own publishing company-The Beginning Publishing Company which she established to assist new and upcoming authors.

Monique is known for her positivity and ability to help women and men alike not only through her books and speaking engagements but through The Worthy Academy, a company she founded to spread the "Know Your Worth" message to youth and adults alike. In her spare time, Mow volunteers at The Worthy Academy, World Shakers Church and New Life International Ministries, Inc.